The Mesa Verde Communities

by Deanne Kells

Table of Contents

Introduction	2
Chapter 1 What Is Mesa Verde?	4
Chapter 2 Who Were the People of Mesa Verde?	8
Chapter 3 What Was Life Like at Mesa Verde?	14
Chapter 4 What Happened to Mesa Verde?	20
Summary	28
Glossary	30
Index	32

Introduction

Mesa Verde is in the United States. People lived at Mesa Verde long ago.

What is Mesa Verde? Who were the people of Mesa Verde? What was their life like? Read to find out.

Words to Know

canyons

communities

Four Corners

kivas

mesa

Mesa Verde

pit houses

Pueblo

valleys

▲ Mesa Verde

See the Glossary on page 30.

3

Chapter 1

What Is Mesa Verde?

Mesa Verde is a **mesa**. A mesa is high land. A mesa is flat land. A mesa has steep sides.

▲ valley

Did You Know?

Mesa Verde means "green table" in Spanish.

Mesa Verde has **canyons**. Canyons are deep **valleys**. Canyons have steep sides.

▼ canyon

▲ A mesa is high land.

Chapter 1

Mesa Verde is in the southwest United States. Mesa Verde is in an area named **Four Corners**.

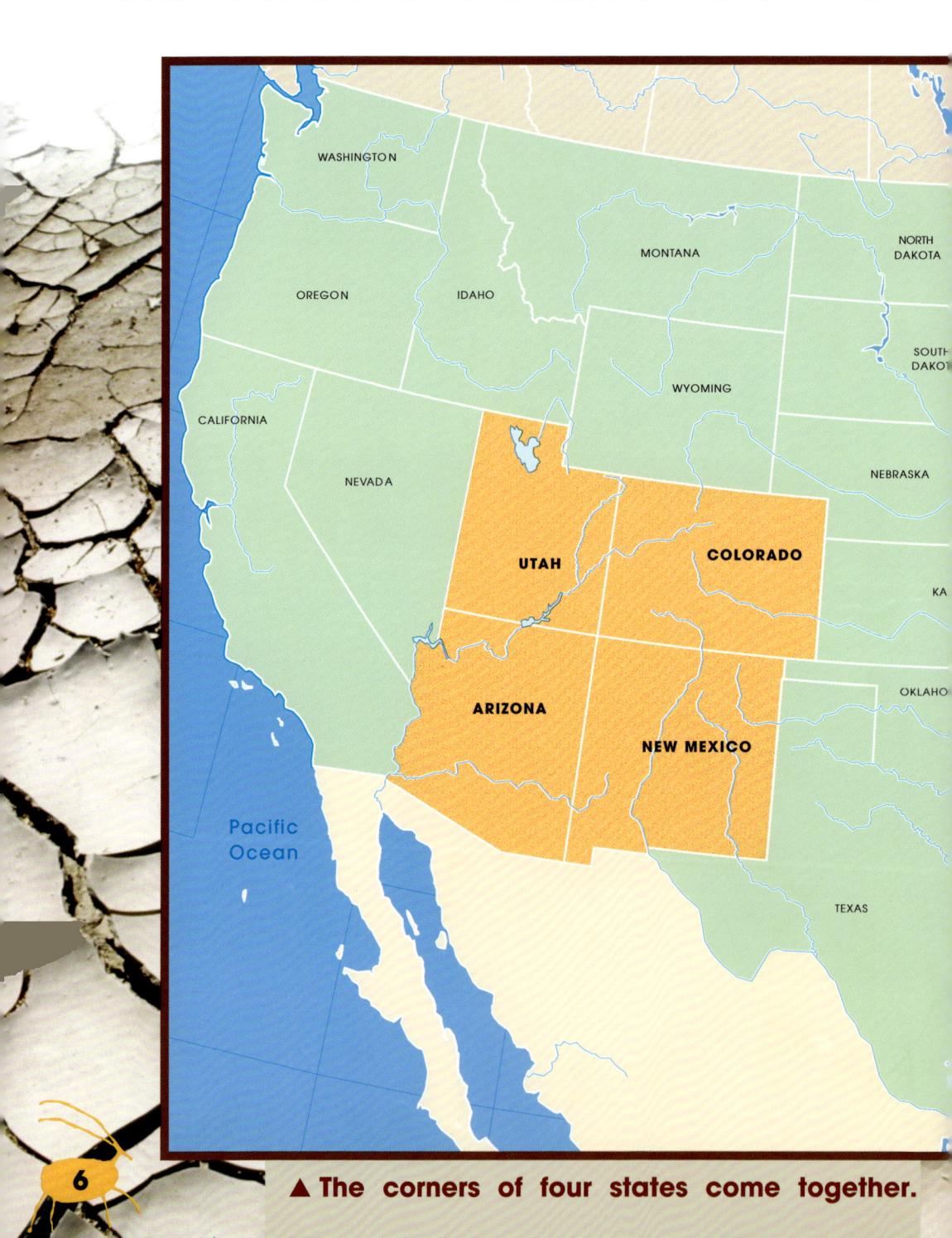

▲ The corners of four states come together.

What Is Mesa Verde?

Figure It Out

What states come together at Four Corners?

Chapter 2

Who Were the People of Mesa Verde?

Native people lived in the Four Corners area. Native people lived there long ago. The native people were the **Pueblo**. Some Pueblo went to Mesa Verde.

▲ Pueblo lived in this community.

The Pueblo people built homes at Mesa Verde. The Pueblo built homes in the ground. These homes were **pit houses**.

▲ A Pueblo pit house was in this place.

It's a Fact
Pueblo is the Spanish word for "town." *Pueblo* is also the name of the people.

Chapter 2

Then the Pueblo built homes on the ground. The homes were made of stone. The homes were in villages, or **communities**. The communities were on the top of the mesa.

▲ The Pueblo lived in this village.

Who Were the People of Mesa Verde?

Most Pueblo communities had **kivas**. Kivas were pits in the ground. Men went into the kivas. Men told stories in the kivas.

> **It's a Fact**
> Women and children did not go into kivas.

▲ This community had many kivas.

Chapter 2

Later the Pueblo built communities in the canyons. The communities were in the sides of canyons. The communities were in cliffs.

Some communities had hundreds of rooms. Some communities looked like one big house.

▲ Cliff Palace was a very large community. It had more than 200 rooms.

Who Were the People of Mesa Verde?

The Pueblo built many communities in the canyons.

▲ Balcony House was a small community.

Chapter 3

What Was Life Like at Mesa Verde?

The Pueblo were hunters. The Pueblo had bows and arrows. The Pueblo hunted for deer and wild turkeys. The Pueblo hunted on top of the mesa.

The Pueblo were farmers. The Pueblo grew crops.

▲ The Pueblo hunted for food.

▲ Pueblo women ground corn.

The Pueblo made tools. The Pueblo made bone tools. The Pueblo made stone tools.

◀ scraper

▲ grinding stone

It's a Fact
The Pueblo used tools to scrape deerskin.

The Pueblo used tools to grind corn.

15

Chapter 3

The Pueblo made pottery. The Pueblo painted the pottery.

The Pueblo used the pottery for cooking. The Pueblo used the pottery for storing things.

▲ The Pueblo made this pottery. ▼

What Was Life Like at Mesa Verde?

The Pueblo made clothes. Sometimes the men made the clothes.

▲ The Pueblo made this cotton shirt.

17

Chapter 3

The Pueblo painted on the canyons. The paintings were about animals. The paintings were about people.

▲ These are Pueblo paintings.

Did You Know?

▲ The Pueblo also made jewelry.

18

What Was Life Like at Mesa Verde?

The Pueblo traded things with other people. The traders walked on paths. The paths were on top of the mesa. The traders went very far.

▲ Traders walked on paths.

Chapter 4

What Happened to Mesa Verde?

Pueblo people lived at Mesa Verde. They lived there for about 800 years. Then the Pueblo went away from Mesa Verde.

▲ The Pueblo went away.

Mesa Verde did not have rain for a long time. The Pueblo did not have water for their crops. The Pueblo did not have water to drink. The Pueblo went away from Mesa Verde.

▲ The crops did not have water.

Chapter 4

Why did the Pueblo go away from Mesa Verde? Where did they go? Scientists think the Pueblo went south. The Pueblo looked for water.

Then no one lived at Mesa Verde. No one lived there for 500 years.

▲ No one lived at Mesa Verde.

What Happened to Mesa Verde?

A man went to Mesa Verde in 1874. The man was William Jackson. Jackson went into a small community. Jackson named the community Two Story Cliff House.

▲ This is the Two Story Cliff House.

Chapter 4

Later, more men went to Mesa Verde. The men found Cliff Palace. The men found other Pueblo communities.

The men took away pieces of pottery. The men took away tools. The men took the things away from the communities.

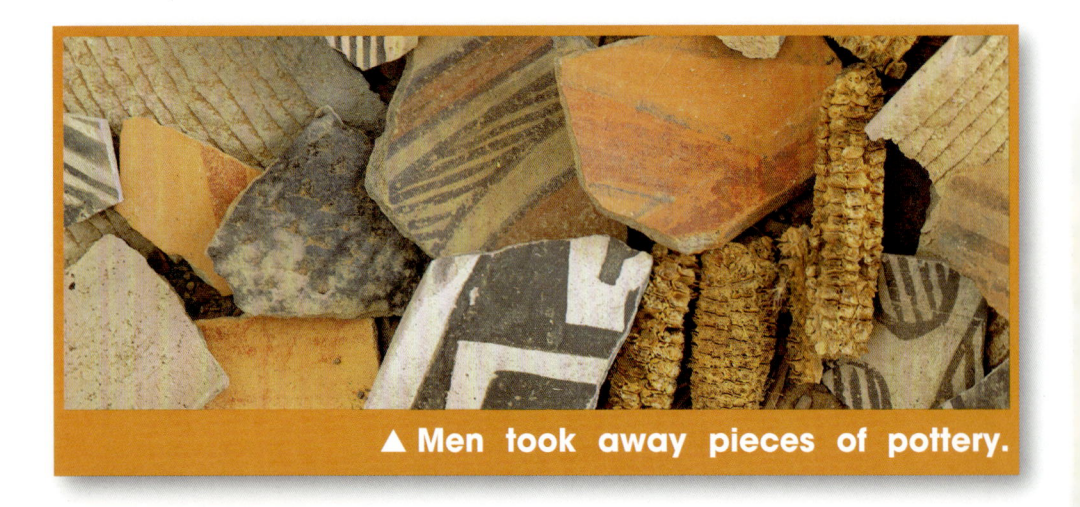

▲ Men took away pieces of pottery.

People to Know

▲ Richard Wetherill found Cliff Palace.

What Happened to Mesa Verde?

More and more people came to Mesa Verde. The people came to see the communities. The people took things away from the communities.

Mesa Verde became a national park in 1906. Then people could not take things from the communities.

Then & Now
Mesa Verde was home to Pueblo people. Now it is a national park.

Solve This
Jackson went to Mesa Verde in 1874. Mesa Verde became a national park in 1906. How many years passed between 1874 and 1906?

Answer: 32 years

Chapter 4

It's a Fact

The Pueblo at Mesa Verde did not have writing. We cannot read about their lives.

The Pueblo did leave things at Mesa Verde. The Pueblo left pottery. The Pueblo left pieces of food. The Pueblo left tools.

What Happened to Mesa Verde?

◀ Scientists found these things at Mesa Verde.

Figure It Out

The Pueblo of Mesa Verde did not have writing. We cannot read about them. How do we know what life was like at Mesa Verde?

Summary

Some Pueblo people lived at Mesa Verde. The Pueblo lived in many communities. The Pueblo went away from Mesa Verde.

What Is Mesa Verde?
- a mesa
- a place with canyons
- a place in the southwestern United States

The Mesa Verde Communities

Who Were the People of Mesa Verde?
- native people
- Pueblo
- people who built pit houses
- people who built communities on top of the ground
- people who built communities in sides of canyons

What Was Life Like at Mesa Verde?
- Pueblo hunted.
- Pueblo grew crops.
- Pueblo made tools.
- Pueblo made pottery.
- Pueblo made clothes.
- Pueblo painted sides of canyons.
- Pueblo traded.

What Happened to Mesa Verde?
- Pueblo went away from Mesa Verde.
- Mesa Verde did not have rain.
- Other people came to Mesa Verde.
- Mesa Verde became a national park.

Think About It

1. What is Mesa Verde?
2. What was life like at Mesa Verde?
3. How do we know what life was like at Mesa Verde?

29

Glossary

canyons deep valleys with steep sides

*Pueblo communities were in the sides of **canyons**.*

communities places where people live and work

*The Pueblo had **communities** at Mesa Verde.*

Four Corners an area in the United States

*Pueblo people lived in the **Four Corners** area.*

kivas pits in the ground used for special times

*Pueblo men went into the **kivas**.*

mesa high land with a flat top

*Mesa Verde is on a **mesa**.*

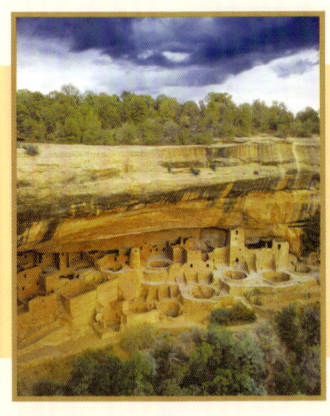

Mesa Verde a large mesa in the United States

*Pueblo people lived at **Mesa Verde**.*

pit houses Pueblo homes built in the ground

*The Pueblo at Mesa Verde had **pit houses**.*

Pueblo native people of the southwestern United States

*Some **Pueblo** lived at Mesa Verde.*

valleys long, low areas of land with hills around them

*There are **valleys** at Mesa Verde.*

Index

Balcony House, 13

bows and arrows, 14

canyons, 5, 12–13, 18, 28–29

Cliff Palace, 12, 24

clothes, 17, 29

communities, 10–13, 24–25, 28

crops, 14, 21, 29

deer, 14–15

farmers, 14

Four Corners, 6–8

homes, 9–10

hunters, 14

kivas, 11

mesa, 4–5, 10, 14, 19, 28

Mesa Verde, 2–6, 8–9, 21–29

national park, 25, 29

paintings, 18

pit houses, 9, 28

pottery, 16, 24, 26, 29

Pueblo, 8–22, 24–29

tools, 15, 24, 26, 29

traders, 19

turkeys, 14

Two Story Cliff House, 23

United States, 2, 6, 28

valleys, 4–5

villages, 10

Wetherill, Richard, 24

writing, 26–27